D0341350

USING THIS BOOK

*One of the best ways of helping children to learn to read is by reading stories to them and with them. This way they learn what **reading** is, and they will gradually come to recognise many words, and begin to read for themselves.*

First, grown-ups read the story on the left-hand pages aloud to the child.

You can reread the story as often as the child enjoys hearing it. Talk about the pictures as you go.

Later the child is encouraged to read the words under the pictures on the right-hand page.

The pages at the back of the book will give you some ideas for helping your child to read.

British Library Cataloguing in Publication Data

McCullagh, Sheila K.
   Look out! It's magic!—(Puddle Lane reading
   programme. Stage 1; v.11)
   1. Readers—1950-
   I. Title   II. Morris, Tony   III. Series
   428.6

   ISBN 0-7214-0913-X

First edition

Published by Ladybird Books Ltd Loughborough Leicestershire UK
Ladybird Books Inc Lewiston Maine 04240 USA

Look out!
It's magic!

written by SHEILA McCULLAGH
illustrated by TONY MORRIS

This book belongs to:

Ladybird Books

Tim and Tessa Catchamouse
lived in a hole, in the steps of
a very old house.
They lived with their mother.
Her name was Pegs.
Most of the old house was empty,
but a magician lived
on the top floor.

Tim and Tessa

One day, Tim and Tessa went
to see the Magician.
They climbed up a tree
that grew near to the house,
and then they jumped on to the roof.
They looked down
through a window in the roof.
The Magician was sitting
in his chair, reading a book.

Tim and Tessa went
to see the Magician.

The Magician looked up, and saw
Tim and Tessa.
"Come down," he said.
"I've been waiting for you.
I've something to show you."
There was a pole leaning
up against the window.
Tim and Tessa
climbed down the pole,
and ran to the Magician.

Tessa and Tim
ran to the Magician.

"Now then," said the Magician.
"Listen to me. Some of the things
in this room are part of my magic.
If you come to see me,
there are some things
you can touch,
and some things which
you mustn't touch."

"I know that," said Tim.

"So do I," said Tessa.

Tessa and Tim and the Magician

There were some cards
on the table.
The Magician picked one up.
"I'm going to write 'No'
on this card," he said.
"If you see this card propped up
against anything, it means
that you mustn't touch it.
It means:
'Look out! It's magic!'"
He pointed to the word
he had written.
"That word is 'No'," he said.

"We'll try and remember,"
said Tim.

No

"Look,"
said the Magician.

13

The Magician picked up
another card.
He wrote 'Yes' on it.
"Look," said the Magician.
"That word is 'Yes'.
If you see that word on something,
it means that it is for you."

"We'll remember **that**,"
said Tessa.

"Look,"
said the Magician.

15

"Now, watch **very** carefully,"
said the Magician.
He picked up two cards.
One was red and one was yellow.
The Magician wrote 'Yes'
on one card, and he wrote
'No' on the other.
He put the cards on the table.
Tim jumped on to the table,
to look at them.

Tim jumped
on to the table.

17

"Put your paw on the card
that says 'Yes',"
said the Magician.
"Red or yellow?"
Tim put his paw
on the red card.

Tim put his paw
on the red card.

There was a flash of red light.
The cards vanished, and
all the bells in the house
started ringing.
Tim jumped off the table
in one big jump, and hid
under the Magician's coat.

Tim jumped
off the table.

"It's all right, Tim,"
said the Magician.
"Don't be frightened."
He snapped his fingers.
The bells stopped ringing.
Tim poked out his head.
"You put your paw on
the 'No' card,"
said the Magician.
"Remember: 'No' means
'Look out! It's magic!'"

"I'll try to remember," said Tim.

Tim and the Magician

"Now you try, Tessa,"
said the Magician.
"Don't be frightened,
I won't let anything hurt you."
He took two more cards.
One was white and
one was yellow.
He wrote 'Yes' on one card,
and 'No' on the other.
He put the cards
on the table.

The Magician put
the cards on the table.

Tessa jumped on to the table.
She looked at the cards
for a long time.
Then she put her paw
on the yellow card.

Tessa put her paw
on the yellow card.

There was a flash of light
and a big bang.
The cards disappeared.
Tessa jumped on to
the Magician's shoulder
and hid.

Tessa jumped.

"It's all right, Tessa,"
said the Magician.
"Don't be frightened.
You touched the card
that says 'No'.
You remember that means,
'Look out! It's magic!'
We'll try once again."
He put Tim and Tessa
on the table.
Then he went to a cupboard,
and took out two bowls.

The Magician
put Tim and Tessa
on the table.

He set the bowls
on the table.
"Now, watch **very** carefully,"
he said.
The Magician took two cards.
One card was red, and
one card was green.
He wrote a word on each card,
and propped one card up
against each bowl.
Tim and Tessa watched him.
"Which card is 'Yes'?"
asked the Magician.

One card was red.
One card was green.

Tim and Tessa
looked at the cards
for a long time.
At last Tim said,
"I **think** the green one
is 'Yes'."

"So do I," said Tessa.
She put her paw
on the green card.

Tessa put her paw
on the green card.

"You're right this time,"
said the Magician.
He snapped his fingers and
all the bells in the house
played a tune.
"Look inside the bowl," he said.
The two little cats looked in.
The bowl was full of milk.
"That's for you,"
said the Magician.
"The card was: 'Yes'."
Tim and Tessa drank
the milk.
It tasted very good.

Tim and Tessa looked.

When Tim and Tessa went home,
they told Pegs all about
the Magician's cards.
"I wish I could make cards like that,"
said Pegs. "Can you remember
the words?"

"I think so," said Tessa.

"I **think** so," said Tim.

"You don't sound very sure,"
said Pegs.

"We'll try very hard to remember,"
said Tim.

Tessa and Tim
and Pegs

Make a simple reading game with the words 'Yes' and 'No'. Take some little boxes (matchboxes will do) and hide a small object in one of them. Write 'No' labels for all the boxes, except the one in which the object is hidden, and write a 'Yes' label for that box.

The game can be made more difficult, by making labels using many of the words from the stories (e.g. Tim, the, cat and so on) and putting them on all the boxes except the one with the 'yes' label.

There are many different ways this kind of game can be played.

Read this to the child:

When Tim and Tessa next
went to see the Magician,
they took some of his cards home.
Pegs found them very useful.
On the next pages, you will see
how she used some of them.

Yes

No

Look at the illustrations, and ask
the child to read the cards. Then ask:
"Why did Pegs put the card on that?"

No

Yes

No

Notes for the parent/teacher

Turn back to the beginning, and print the child's name in the space on the title page, using ordinary, not capital letters.

Now go through the book again. Look at each picture and talk about it. Point to the caption below, and read it aloud yourself.

Run your finger along under the words as you read, so that the child learns that reading goes from left to right.

Encourage the child to read the words under the illustrations. Don't rush in with the word before he/she has had time to think, but don't leave him/her struggling.

Read this story as often as the child likes hearing it. The more opportunities he/she has of looking at the illustrations and **reading** the captions with you, the more he/she will come to recognise the words.

If you have several books, let the child choose which story he/she would like.

"No.
"I live in the M____
at the end of Puddle Lane.
But I always come here on Fridays.
They have cheese and nuts
in the market on Fridays.
Come and see."

Jeremy looked down.
He looked at one of the tables.
There was a big cheese
at one end of the table,
and a basket of nuts
at the other end.

Jeremy looked down.

17